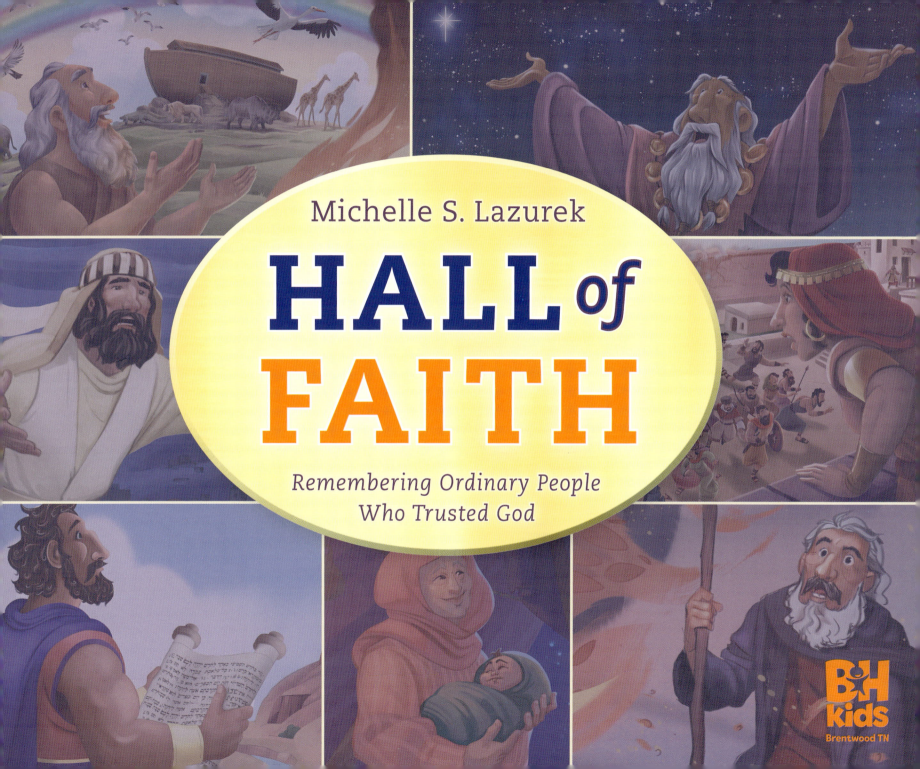

To Caleb and Leah

May you have faith that God can be trusted all the days of your life.

Copyright © 2024 by Michelle S. Lazurek.
Author is represented by the literary
agency of Credo Communications LLC,
Grand Rapids, Michigan,
www.credocommunications.net
Art Copyright © 2024 by B&H Publishing
Group, Brentwood, Tennessee.
Dewey Decimal Classification: C234.2
Subject Heading: BIBLE. N.T.
HEBREWS 11 \ FAITH \ TRUST
ISBN: 978-1-4300-9643-6
Printed in Shenzhen, Guangdong, China,
in April 2024
1 2 3 4 5 6 • 28 27 26 25 24

The Bible is bursting with stories of people who took big risks to obey God.

The book of Hebrews calls this **faith.** Faith is believing that God can be trusted even when we can't see Him working.

Having faith can be hard! But the Bible says lots of people have been putting their faith in God for a long time.

God asked Abel and his brother Cain to bring their best offerings to Him.

Abel had faith even when his brother Cain did not. He believed **God can be trusted.** Abel is remembered for being a man of great faith.

God asked Noah to build a big boat, or an ark, to keep Noah's family and many animals safe during a flood God would send to the earth.

Noah had faith. When the flood came, God kept them safe. By faith, Noah believed **God can be trusted!**

God promised Sarah she would give birth to a son. At first, Sarah laughed at God's promise. She was too old to have a baby! But **Sarah had faith,** and she had a baby boy named Isaac. God fulfilled His promise to Sarah because **God can be trusted.**

God asked Abraham to give his son as a sacrifice. Isaac was the son God had promised Abraham and his wife Sarah. Abraham was given a difficult task, but **he had faith because God can be trusted.** He was willing to sacrifice his son. God saw Abraham's faith and gave him a ram to sacrifice instead.

God promised that His people would live in a special land. Even though Joseph and his family had to leave that land, **Joseph had faith** and believed **God can be trusted.** He believed God would do what He said He would do, even when he couldn't see Him doing it.

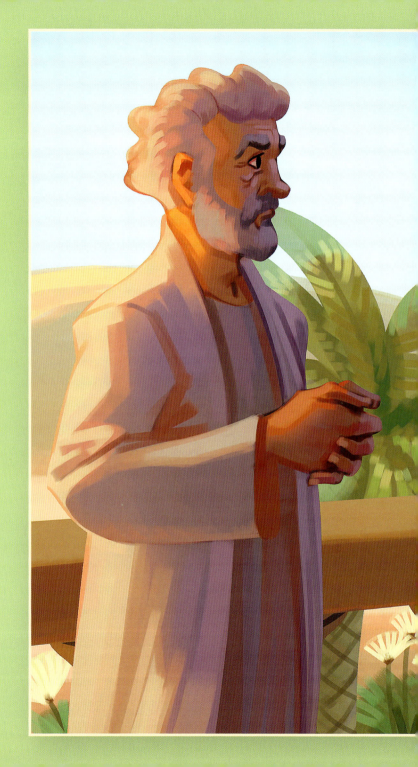

God asked Moses to demand Pharaoh set God's people free from slavery. Moses was scared. He told God to send someone else. He didn't know that God can be trusted.

Eventually, Moses had faith, and he led the people out of Egypt toward God's Promised Land.

God told Joshua and his great army to march quietly around Jericho's tall walls for seven days.

They might have looked funny marching, but God can be trusted. Joshua and the Israelites had faith. Because of their faith, the walls of the city fell!

Rahab welcomed Joshua's friends into her house, even though they were her people's enemies. **Rahab had faith.** She chose to side with God's people instead of her own.

Rahab's choice was risky, but **God can be trusted.** Because of her faith, God protected Rahab and her family when the walls of Jericho fell.

Samuel heard God call him one night when he was a boy. **Samuel had faith** and answered God.

When Samuel grew up, he anointed David as the new king of Israel. Even though David wasn't who the Israelites wanted to be king at first, **Samuel had faith** because he believed **God can be trusted.**

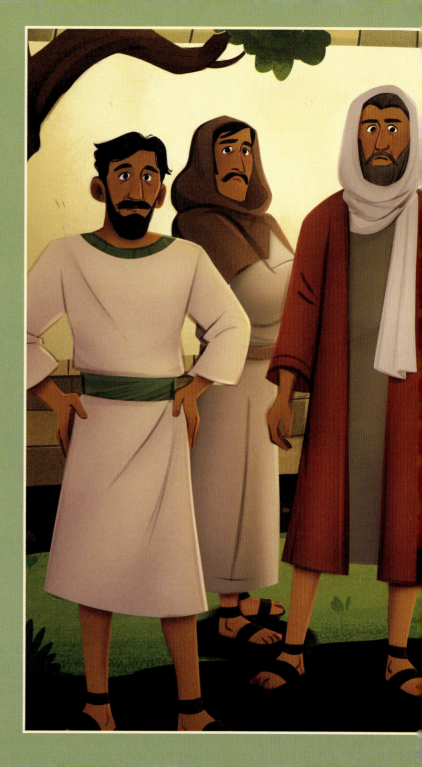

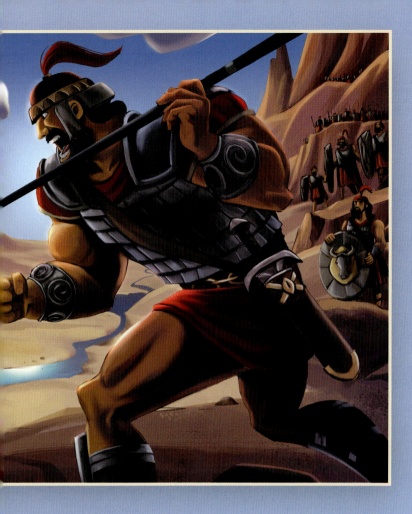

God chose David to become the next king of Israel! **David had faith.** When David was just a boy, he defeated a huge man named Goliath with nothing but a rock and a slingshot. Though everyone else was scared, David knew **God can be trusted.**

As king, **David had faith.** He loved and trusted God so much that he ruled God's people with strength and mercy. Because of his humility, God called David "the man after His own heart." What an honor!

God called the prophets to deliver His messages to God's people. **The prophets had faith.** Sometimes their messages gave people hope. Sometimes their messages made people mad.

But **God can be trusted.** By faith, the people who obeyed the prophets' words received God's protection.

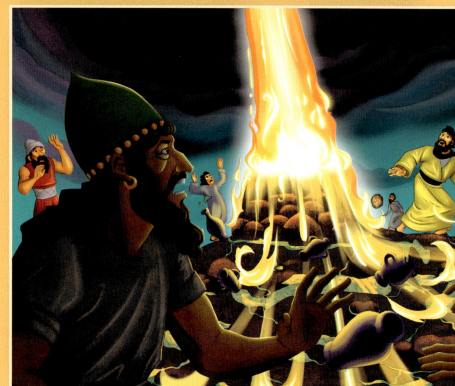

These people, and many more, are members of the Bible's Hall of Faith in Hebrews 11. **They had faith** even though people made fun of them. They defeated armies, risked their lives, fought for justice, and went where God told them to because they believed **God can be trusted.** They had hope that God would do the biggest thing He promised: send a Savior to rescue His people!

People who have faith point to the true hero of the Bible: Jesus. Jesus is the Savior whom God promised to send. He lived a perfect life, died on the cross, and rose from the dead.

Jesus always spoke truth, led His followers by faith, answered when His Father called Him, welcomed people into His kingdom, and sacrificed Himself for our sins. Jesus is God, and He is the One we put our **faith** in!

Did you know you can have faith too? When you have faith, you believe in Jesus and give your life to Him!

God can be trusted even when we can't see Him working. We can obey God like the people in the Hall of Faith.

Remember:

Now faith is confidence in what we hope for and assurance about what we do not see.
—Hebrews 11:1 NIV

Read:

The heroes in the Hall of Faith did not have any special abilities or look a certain way. They simply had faith in God. They obeyed Him in whatever He asked them to do and let God do the rest. They were like baseball MVPs who have their names listed in the Hall of Fame.

Look back through the Hall of Faith and read about the people God chose to use. Pick a few you would like to learn more about and read about them in the Bible. Discuss something new you learned. In what ways could you be like them? How do they remind you of Jesus?

Think:

1. What do you think it looks like to have faith in God? Can you name someone in your life who demonstrates faith?

2. Do you have a favorite person from the Hall of Faith? Why was that person your choice?

3. What were some ways God was faithful during that person's difficult situation?

4. God speaks to us in many ways. Have you ever heard from God? What was it like? If not, what do you think it would be like?

5. What is something God might call you to do? Make friends with someone who is lonely? Invite someone to church? Volunteer in your community? How will you demonstrate your faith in God?